LANDSCAPE PHOTOGRAPHY

LANDSCAPE

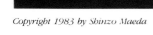

PHOTOGRAPHY

INTRODUCTORY ESSAY BY GENE THORNTON

AMPHOTO
AMERICAN PHOTOGRAPHIC BOOK PUBLISHING
AN IMPRINT OF WATSON-GUPTILL PUBLICATIONS/NEW YORK

First published 1984 in New York by American Photographic Book
Publishing: an imprint of Watson-Guptill Publications,
a division of Billboard Publications, Inc.,
1515 Broadway, New York, NY 10036

Library of Congress Catalog Card Number: 84-45062
ISBN 0-8174-4154-9

Distributed in the United Kingdom by Phaidon Press, Ltd.,
Littlegate House, St. Ebbe's St., Oxford

Manufactured in Japan
1 2 3 4 5 6 7 8 9 / 89 88 87 86 85 84

Edited by Don Earnest and Marisa Bulzone
Designed by Jay Anning
Graphic Production by Katherine Rosenbloom

CONTENTS

THE NEW ART OF LANDSCAPE PHOTOGRAPHY

by Gene Thornton

The landscape is a rich and varied subject for the camera. From the rugged grandeur of alpine mountains to the peaceful calm of lakes and lawns, from the intricate delicacy of flowering trees to the bare, abstract beauty of desert dunes, it presents the photographer with a range and variety of subject matter unsurpassed by any other feature of the visible world.

A landscape of some sort is always available in a way that most other subjects—people, for instance—are not. For most photographers it is as close as the nearest window, and susceptible to a wide range of treatments, from the realistic to the very nearly abstract, from the coolly objective to the intensely personal, from the poetic to the documentary.

As a subject for photography, landscape is as old as the medium itself. The first workable photographic process was daguerreotypy, and some of Daguerre's first successful pictures were views of the streets and buildings of Paris. Then, within months after the process was introduced, daguerreotypists were at work photographing scenery and monuments not only in

Gene Thornton is a renowned author and lecturer on the subject of photography. He is the photo critic for the New York Times, *and author of the book* Masters of the Camera *(Holt, Reinhart & Winston).*

LUCANIA (BASILICATA) REGION, SOUTHERN ITALY. *Copyright 1984 by Franco Fontana*

WINTER MOUNTAINS, MONTANA. *Copyright 1984 by Sonja Bullaty*

Paris but as far away as Egypt, Russia, and America. Their process was too slow to capture motion, and it could not reproduce the colors of nature, two disappointing features of early photography that were much noted and commented upon when the medium was new. However, it was well suited to subjects that did not move, and from that day to the present, landscape has been a fascinating subject for the photographer.

Today when most people think of landscape photography they think first of the classic photographs of Ansel Adams and Edward Weston, and rightly so. These men were among the pioneers of modern landscape photography, and most photographers working in the field today owe them a debt. After them, people may think of the great 19th century expedition and travel photographers: Timothy O'Sullivan and William Henry Jackson among the pioneering explorer-photographers of the American West; Samuel Bourne, John Thomson, and William Brad-

ford among the Europeans who travelled to India, China, the Arctic, and all over the world to record strange sights and unfamiliar places with their medium's matchless fidelity to appearances. These men continued the tradition—as old as photography itself, and still very much alive today in the age of mass tourism and space exploration—of taking the camera wherever men can go and bringing back pictures of things that those at home would otherwise not see.

The differences in motive between these two groups of photographers, the 19th century explorer-photographers like O'Sullivan and the 20th century artist-photographers like Adams, is great and striking. By and large the 19th century photographers were scientists and reporters, concentrating on places and things that had never been properly recorded before, and aiming primarily for absolute clarity and accuracy of presentation. When they photographed a bit of Western landscape it was, first of all, to show its geo-

WHITE BIRCH IN AUTUMN, CONNECTICUT. *Copyright 1984 by Angelo Lomeo*

logical structure; to show, for instance, Yosemite Valley as an example of the shapes glaciers carve when they move down mountain valleys.

The 20th century masters, on the other hand, were first of all conscious artists, more interested in beauty and expression than in documentation. When Ansel Adams focused on Yosemite in a snow storm he saw it not as a textbook example of glacial action but as a symbol of the grandeur and nobility of nature.

Despite these differences, however, the two groups had much in common. Both did their best and most characteristic work with view cameras mounted on tripods and a very limited array of lenses, and both worked almost exclusively in black and white. There was even some convergence of motive. The 19th century scientist-photographers, though not primarily interested in artistic effect, did not ignore it. William Henry Jackson, for instance, often worked side by side with the painter

Thomas Moran, asking his advice on selection of subject and composition. Similarly, the 20th century artist-photographers, though not documentarians or reporters, had a scrupulous regard for facts. They did not approve of rearranging nature to make it more interesting or more beautiful, and Edward Weston was severely criticized by his colleagues for placing a sea shell on the rocks of Point Lobos to make a composition more dramatic.

Though today's landscape photographers owe much to their 19th and early 20th century predecessors, two technical innovations of the mid-20th century have made great changes in the art. One is the development of the 35mm camera with its wide range of interchangeable lenses. The other is the development of modern color film processes.

When hand-held cameras became readily available in the 1920s, photographers went on an orgy of experiment, snapping away at every visible object from every conceivable point of view and in every possible light.

WHITE SANDS NATIONAL MONUMENT. *Copyright 1984 by Harald Sund*

MINGSHA DUNES, CHINA. *Copyright 1984 by Yuan Li*

They went too far, perhaps, but once the novelty wore off, photography was left with a new flexibility of composition and approach.

Something similar started in the 1940s when new advances in film made color photography outside the studio easy even for casual amateurs. People went around snapping everything that had lots and lots of color, the more color the better. It took a while for the excitement to die down to the point where color could be used for a purpose.

When, however, both of these innovations had been absorbed, a new type of landscape photography emerged that is the subject of this book. In composition it is freer and less formal than the classic photography of the past. And it was, from the very beginning, conceived in color.

The eight landscape photographers whose works are shown in this book do not constitute a school, such as the *F/64* Group that claimed Edward Weston as a member. That is to say, they are not a close-knit group of artists from the same area who share common goals and work in the same style. Most of them do not even know one another. Franco Fontana was born, and still lives, in Italy. Shinzo Maeda has spent all his life in Japan. Three of the American photographers were born and grew up in other countries: Sonja Bullaty in Czechoslovakia, Yuan Li in China, and John Chang McCurdy in Korea. Of the three native-born Americans, Harald Sund and Steven C. Wilson are from the West Coast, while Angelo Lomeo was born, and still lives, in New York City.

These eight photographers also occupy different places in the photographic community. Five of them—Sonja Bullaty, Angelo Lomeo, John Chang McCurdy, Harald Sund, and Steven C. Wilson—are globe-trotting professionals whose assignments keep them moving from one part of the world to another and at times take them out of the field of landscape. Two of them, Franco Fontana and Shinzo Maeda, began as amateurs, and only later achieved professional status. One, Yuan Li, is still an amateur in the sense that he makes his living in a field other than photography.

All, however, have achieved widespread public recognition, and despite many differences in style and approach, they have several things in common, the first of which is the fact that they all love to photograph landscape.

"I cannot imagine *not* photographing the landscape," says Sonja Bullaty, though she also photographs people, cities, industry, and art; and the others share her feeling. Shinzo Maeda has never photographed anything but landscape. Franco Fontana has only recently begun to turn his attention to other subjects. For Yuan Li, Angelo Lomeo, and Harald Sund, it was the love of landscape that led them to photography. "My interest in photography began when I traveled across the country in one of those typical summer excursions taken by many Americans, visiting national parks and fabled Western towns," says Li. He was so impressed by the "awesome" landscape of the West that he decided to learn photography in order to express his feelings about it.

Another thing that all eight photographers have in common is the use of color. "Color has not been my choice; it has chosen me," says Franco Fontana, and Yuan Li agrees. "The world is full of color," he says. "Why should I make it artificially black and white?" "In earlier years," says Angelo Lomeo, "I photographed in black and white, and it was an extremely important discipline and good training. But the world is a colorful place and therefore I choose to work in color."

Some of these photographers do not, in fact, have time to do anything else. "I've done black and white, and I loved it, but I don't have time for the darkroom," says Harald Sund. Steven Wilson agrees. "Color lab men are competent and reliable. And I don't have to go white-skinned and bug-eyed fiddling with my exposures." Shinzo Maeda has another reason for preferring color. "Black-and-white photography is no longer popular in Japan. It doesn't make enough profit in business."

A third thing all eight photographers have in common is the use of modern equipment that gives them great freedom and flexibility of approach. Except for Shinzo Maeda, who favors large-format view cameras, and John Chang McCurdy, who prefers the 2¼-inch square format, they all use 35mm single-lens-reflex cameras, and most of them use a wide range of lenses, depending on what kind of picture they have in mind and what the subject requires. The modern tripods most of them use on occasion are much more flexible instruments than the tripods used by 19th century photographers, and some, like Harald Sund, Steven Wilson, and Yuan Li, always use one. "A tripod turns almost any camera into a precision instrument," says Sund. "It enables you to achieve more control over composition and take full advantage of your equipment's potential for speed and sharpness."

There is one more thing that these eight photographers share, not only with each other, but with the photographic masters of the past: a conviction that a good landscape photograph is something more than a mere record of appearances. "It is very important for a photographer to have a philosophical view about life," says Shinzo Maeda, "because personal character is reflected in the work." Yuan Li thinks that a successful piece of work must project the impression that the photographer is in "full control" of what is in the photograph. "Without emphasis or individual interpretations," he says, "landscape can often be bland." For Franco Fontana, photography is "emotional, spontaneous." Using photography, he says, "I transfer my inner expression through creative and subjective means." As Sonja Bullaty puts it, "Photography is the expression of one's true self, and the best images are the result of an inner response to the world around one. One's whole life precedes the moment one pushes the shutter."

In practice what this means is that each photographer starts out with a personal conception of what a landscape photograph should be, a conception that determines what sort of subject he will seek out to photograph and how he will photograph it. These conceptions are deeply personal and differ from one photographer to another. What interests Angelo Lomeo is what he refers to as the "sheer perfection" of nature's design. "I marvel at its abstraction," he says. Franco Fontana has a related idea, though his pictures are very different. He is attracted to the forms and colors of landscape, "like a space suspended, without time." Steven Wilson, by way of contrast, is a biologist whose main interest is in showing the relationship between wildlife and the natural environment. "Perhaps I'm bought by some clients as a *landscape photographer*," he says, "but that's because I put on the wide-angle lens and *back off* visually to show relationships."

Though each photographer approaches the landscape with a personal idea, "each landscape is a different situation to be solved," says Angelo Lomeo, and all eight photographers agree that the photographer cannot simply impose a solution on it. "Once I find a general area that appeals to me, I usually allow the scene to determine my photograph," says Yuan Li. "I approach the landscape as an observer and interpreter, rather than as a dictator or master." Steven Wilson puts the matter more bluntly. "A pre-conceived idea usually gets scuttled when exposed to the intricacies of reality. The mechanics of photography require that research information, intuitive reaction, science, craftsmanship, and art all meet at the instant of exposure. It is not an easy trick we attempt."

Good landscape photographers are always on the lookout for locations that will give them the kind of picture they want, and when they find one they may, like Harald Sund, try to imagine what it would look like at different times of day or year and under different lighting and weather conditions. Sund is a great believer in advance planning to reduce uncertainty and accident. When he is scouting locations he is always thinking about what point of view, lens, exposure, and so on would best capture what he wants. If he plans to photograph a specific subject he researches it in advance. Thus, if he wants to photograph the full moon over the ocean at high tide, he consults a calendar and a tide table to find the time and date when the two coincide.

How much and what kind of equipment a landscape photographer should take on location depends on what kind of work he anticipates doing. Franco Fontana and Yuan Li prefer zoom lenses when photographing landscape, but most of the others use a wide range of lenses, with their choice determined by the requirements of the subject and situation.

Whether or not they use filters, all of the eight express a desire to capture nature's colors as they are, without falsification. "I use no filters of any type," says Franco Fontana, "because I have no use for them. In nature colors exist in all their completeness; filters damage those colors." Sonja Bullaty occasionally uses a filter "to emphasize existing colors," and Steven Wilson uses 2 × 2 gels "maybe a fourth of the time" for balancing light, though he never uses filters "to substantially change light."

NUANCES. *Copyright 1984 by John Chang McCurdy*

Photographers like Sund and Wilson, who often spend days or weeks in the field far from their home base and normal sources of supply, take everything that they might need with them—not just cameras and film but whatever other equipment they normally use. In these circumstances back packs are essential, and Wilson has several, each designed for a different climate and environment. Sonja Bullaty and Angelo Lomeo usually work as a team and consequently are able to share equipment. But even so, they have fitted the trunk of their automobile for use as a big camera bag. Yuan Li, however, finds that too much equipment hampers him and causes him to lose the fun and spontaneity of photography. He now owns and uses two cameras, but until recently he did all his work with one.

If these photographers have a *least* favorite season for photographing landscape, it is summer. Most of them find autumn, winter, and spring more varied and interesting. And if they have a *least* favorite time of day, it is midday. Most of them prefer to photograph early in the morning or late in the afternoon, in the hours just before and after sunrise and sunset. They find the light warmer then and the shadows more clearly defined. Beyond that, however, there is no general agreement. Franco Fontana finds that days with clear skies and strongly contrasting light are ideal for his type of work. Sonja Bullaty and Shinzo Maeda often prefer an overcast day for added color saturation.

All agree, however, that light is a challenging factor in landscape photography, since it is not the actual landscape that imprints its image on the film, but the light reflected from the landscape. "Landscapes are never the same twice," says Sonja Bullaty. "It is the light that changes them and gives them a new meaning every time." Unlike the studio photographer, who can adjust his lights until he gets the effect he wants, the landscape photographer has no control over his light. "If the light is not right I try to wait for it," says Angelo Lomeo, "or, if I can, I return as many times as necessary until conditions *are* right."

These eight landscape photographers have many things in common with their 19th and 20th century predecessors. Like the great explorer-photographers of the 19th century, some of them travel to remote and relatively unknown parts of the world, bringing back pictures of places and things that most people would otherwise not see. Like the artist-photographers of the early 20th century, some of them find beauty and inspiration in ordinary things that others might pass by. However, their use of modern color materials and the handier, more flexible equipment of modern photography help them take pictures that are in many ways very different from those of the masters of the past.

The lack of color in 19th and early 20th century photography meant that photographs were conceived primarily in terms of light and shadow as opposed to either local or atmospheric color. However, today's color films and papers make it possible to conceive and take pictures in which contrasts or harmonies of color are the building blocks of design. Shinzo Maeda's lyrical photographs of autumn leaves and Harald Sund's sinister sunsets would lose most of their point in black and white, while the contrast in colors between man-made objects and nature adds greatly to Angelo Lomeo's witty "road-sign" landscapes. Some of John Chang McCurdy's photographs have very little contrast between dark and light—without color, the difference between one part and another would be scarcely visible. Others, though very close to monochromatic, make their point through subtle shifts of color.

The great flexibility made possible by lightweight modern equipment and faster, cheaper, more convenient film has also led to changes in the way that landscape is conceived and composed. The large format view cameras of 19th century landscape photographers often had only one medium-angle lens, and their large collodion wet plates had to be sensitized just before exposure and developed soon afterwards, the whole process sometimes taking upwards of an hour. Since it was much more difficult and time-consuming to take a photograph then than it is today, far fewer exposures were made, and those that were made were usually far more conventional in composition and approach. Telescopic or wide-angle views were rare, while unusual framing and unexpected angles of vision were on the whole avoided in favor of straightforward classical composition (the best general view from the most revealing angle).

This classic approach to landscape continued to be the rule through the generation of Ansel Adams and Edward Weston, both of whom used large-format view cameras, though their negative materials were faster and easier to use than those of their 19th century predecessors. Today, however, with a wide range of lenses, photographers can zoom in or back away from their subject without moving the camera, while smaller, more portable cameras have encouraged the use of eccentric framing and unusual points of view. Yuan Li and Franco Fontana base much of their approach to landscape on the use of the zoom lens to isolate and flatten a distant bit of landscape and bring it closer to the viewer. Steven Wilson, on the other hand, often uses a wide-angle lens to back off from a subject and bring a great deal more of the surrounding landscape into the picture than would be possible with a 19th century landscape lens. Harald Sund and Sonja Bullaty often use a classic approach to composition, while John Chang McCurdy and Shinzo Maeda characteristically emphasize pattern and color in a more abstract way.

In every case, however, the aim is the same: to communicate to the viewer the experience of the landscape that the photographer has had. Yuan Li feels that a photograph should have "a universal and timeless appeal, enlightening viewers of different backgrounds and different generations with individual meaning." Angelo Lomeo sums it up quite nicely. "When a picture turns out the way I first saw it in my head, when I can show others something they may not have seen for themselves, then I am happy with my work."

FOREST FIRE, VANCOUVER, BRITISH COLUMBIA. *Copyright 1984 by Steven C. Wilson/ENTHEOS*

HARALD SUND

The drama, sometimes even the violence of nature is a prominent feature of the landscape photographs of Harald Sund shown on the following pages. In one, a jagged bolt of lightning turns the night sky orange. In another, a crescent moon hangs over the smoking crater of Mount St. Helens while, in the foreground, steam rises out of a wasteland of rocky rubble. In a third, ice breaking free from the face of a tidewater glacier makes an explosive black cloud against the unearthly blue of the glacier.

Even when all is calm there is a touch of theater in these pictures. Gigantic rocky pinnacles are silhouetted between blood red sunsets and the sea. Huge thunderheads rise up into dark skies over waters still as glass. Or a hazy moon is reflected in mirror-like waters out of which rise eerie spires like the towers of an underwater cathedral.

Not all of Harald Sund's photographs are such dramatic presentations of nature. Though he is best known for his nature and travel photographs, he is a successful commercial photographer who takes on many different kinds of assignments for magazines, books and corporate reports—"everything," he says, "except weddings and bar mitzvahs." However, it was Sund's love of nature, formed in the spectacular scenery of the Pacific Northwest, that led him to photography.

He grew up in Seattle in a house that had sunset views of the Olympic Mountains. His parents were outdoor people who took him camping and fishing during his youth, and he took advantage of the region's many opportunities for sailing and skiing. While in his early twenties he tried some studio photography without any great interest or success. Then, when he was twenty-four he climbed Mount Rainier with a photographer friend who was also a world class mountain climber, and when he saw his friend's photographs of the climb he immediately realized that he wanted to spend his life doing this kind of photography.

Sund is basically self taught—an advantage, he thinks, because he was never tempted to emulate an instructor. He does feel that his brief studio experience gave him an understanding of lighting, control of the picture field, and presentation of product. However, though his technical ability has increased over the years, he feels that his style has not. "My ability to react and judge things is faster, so that I can get the same results in less time," he says. "But the way I see and feel about nature is the same. I think the way people see is innate and unique. I doubt if anyone can be trained to see if the innate ability is lacking." His work has appeared in *Life, Holiday, Audubon Magazine, Modern Photography*, the *Reader's Digest Book of Christmas* and numerous publications of Time-Life Books in addition to corporate publications like AT&T's *Bell Magazine* and Exxon's *The Lamp*.

Harald Sund likes photographing in black and white, but he no longer has time for the dark room work, and now photographs exclusively in color. His film of preference is Kodachrome 64, and his usual camera is a Canon F1 with a wide range of lenses. He uses polarizing and neutral density filters on occasion, and he likes to use a tripod both because it makes more careful composition possible, and because it enables him to shoot slow for sharpness. His favorite light is the light just before and just after sunrise and sunset, and he photographs at every time of the year—"even in winter in Alaska," he says, "when the temperature is 59 degrees below zero by the thermometer with a wind chill factor of more than 100 degrees below."

The areas that Sund likes to photograph best are the Pacific Northwest where he grew up, the American Southwest for its varied scenery and national parks, and Alaska. However, as a successful commercial photographer he gets all kinds of assignments, some quite different from the kind he likes best. He does not feel that this hampers him in his own work. On the contrary, he finds that an unfamiliar or uninteresting subject stimulates thought that carries over into other work.

Though he naturally takes advantage of accidents, he leaves as little as possible to chance. To capture the dramatic lightning flash on page 27 he needed good luck, but he was waiting for the luck when it occurred, his camera at the ready and pointing toward the sector of the sky where the lightning was flashing. When he is scouting locations he is always thinking about how the location would look under different light and weather conditions, and what would be the best point of view, lens, aperture, and so on to get what he wants. If he wants a picture of the full moon over the ocean at high tide, he does not just wait for it to happen, he consults a tide table and a calendar to find out when in advance. "For every visual problem there is a visual solution," he says—even if it means crawling through mud or getting up at three o'clock in the morning.

MONO LAKE, CALIFORNIA

Copyright 1984 by Harald Sund. Canon F-1, Kodachrome 64, 24mm lens, 5 sec. at f/8
The mirror-like waters of Mono Lake reflect a hazy moon, just one hour after sunset, and support eerie spired forms that strongly resemble the towers of an underwater cathedral. This is one part—albeit a marvelously strange part—of Harald Sund's world.

NEAR DENALI NATIONAL PARK, ALASKA

Copyright 1984 by Harald Sund. Canon F-1, Kadachrome 64, 24mm lens, 1/250 sec. at f/8
Cumulus clouds scarcely positioned above ground level are reflected in all their powerful glory in the crystal clear waters of an Alaskan lake. Turn the photograph upside down and the image is practically identical—a Rorshach test, of sorts. Sund always seeks, and finds, drama in nature.

Preceding page
COLUMBIA GLACIER, PRINCE WILLIAM SOUND, VALDEZ, ALASKA

Copyright 1984 by Harald Sund. Canon F-1, Kodachrome 64, 135mm lens, 1/500 sec. at f/8
Ice breaking free from the face of a tidewater glacier explodes violently into a huge black cloud against the unearthly blue of the glacier. The overall effect is certainly dramatic, and further heightened by the layers of various textures, shapes, and shades of blue.

MOUNT ST. HELENS, WASHINGTON

Copyright 1984 by Harald Sund. Canon F-1, Kodachrome 64, 20mm lens, 1 sec. at f/11
In the background, a white speck of a moon looms over the
smoking crater of Mount St. Helens; in the foreground, steam rises
out of a wasteland of rocky rubble. Mysterious in its desolation,
this landscape could just as easily be that of a distant planet
as of this earth.

Overleaf

BOHEMIAN FOREST, BAVARIA, GERMANY

Copyright 1984 by Harald Sund. Canon F-1, Kodachrome 64, 24mm lens, 1/250 sec. at f/8
An hour or so after the sun has risen, its light gently filters
through the lines of tall and delicate trees, adding a gentle
shimmer to the reflections in the water. Sund's graphic instincts
are expressed beautifully in a photograph that is painterly
in both style and mood.

HAWAII

Copyright 1984 by Harald Sund. Canon F-1, Kodachrome 64, 135mm lens, 1/250 sec. at f/8

Clouds passing above the Pacific create an almost monochromatic
image of impressive impact. Taken three hours before sunset
while the skies were darkened by a storm, one glimmer of light
managed to pass through and strike the still waters like the
vertical slash of a finely tuned blade.

ARKANSAS

Copyright 1984 by Harald Sund. Canon F-1, Kodachrome 64, 200mm lens, Bulb at f/5.6

In this photograph, Sund creates an image that gives expression to the biblical reference to angry heavens. A jagged bolt of lightning sets the night skies above Arkansas ablaze with vivid color depicting a force so strong that one can almost hear the thunder.

OREGON COAST, NEAR LINCOLN CITY

Copyright 1984 by Harald Sund. Pentax, Kodachrome 64, 135mm lens, 1/30 sec. at f/11

A gigantic rocky pinnacle is silhouetted between delicately colored
sunset skies and a calm blue sea. The dividing line between sky
and water could not have been straighter if Sund had pencilled
it in himself. There is a feeling of anticipation beyond the
calm in this photograph—a sense of expectation as with the
calm before the storm.

CANNON BEACH, OREGON

Copyright 1984 by Harald Sund. Canon F-1, Kodachrome 64, 100mm lens, 2 sec. at f/11
More rocky pinnacles against a sky, and jutting up from a sea,
of an artist's palette of reds and purples. A very dramatic photograph of forms ancient in character; like many of Sund's photographs, it readily brings to mind images of a lost world and
a forgotten time.

MAUI, HAWAII

Copyright 1984 by Harald Sund. Canon F-1, Kodachrome 64, 35mm lens, Bulb (15 sec.) at f/8
Though heavy fog at dusk softens the images and mutes the
colors, the eerie light and peculiar shapes give rise to an impression of impending doom. Or is it a sense of overwhelming calm?
Sund's photographs often depict a landscape so unusual that
interpretation becomes a confounding, yet fascinating, exercise.

Opposite page

NORTHERN OREGON COAST

Copyright 1984 by Harald Sund. Canon F-1, Kodachrome 64, 35mm lens, Bulb (4 sec.) at f/5.6
The presence of life in a place as desolate as this depicts an image
of survival. The deep, beautiful purples of sky and water reinforce
the rather spiritual message of this photograph, and, of course,
highlight Sund's extraordinary use of color.

YUAN LI

The starkly simple landscapes of Yuan Li often convey a sense of mankind's smallness and insignificance in the face of nature. In several pictures in the following portfolio, a manmade structure—a barn, a wind mill, a pylon carrying power lines—is contrasted with rolling hills or fields seen under a raking light. Each of these structures is an instrument of man's control over nature, but in Li's photographs each is dwarfed by its natural setting.

A similar view of man's place in nature is suggested by the opening photograph of a desert seen from the edge of an oasis. Tall trees, almost black, frame a zigzag line of sand dunes receding in the late afternoon sunlight toward a low peak, above which a pale moon hangs, a reminder of the night soon to come. Poets have often spoken of life as an oasis in a desert or a brief day bounded by night, and both metaphors are given visual expression in this photograph.

"There is a certain metaphoric connection between landscape and the inner self of a human being," says Li, and what he tries to do in his photographs is give it expression. In so doing he is drawing on his oriental roots. Though he now lives in the United States, Yuan Li was born on the mainland of China and brought up on Taiwan. He came to the United States to do graduate work in physics, receiving a Ph.D. in 1966 from the University of Indiana, and is now an associate professor of physics at Rutgers University in New Jersey.

As a teenager he was attracted to Chinese classical poetry and painting, which often uses landscape to convey philosophical ideas, and through photography he seeks to do the same thing. In 1969, on a summer vacation trip through the national parks and historic old towns of the West, he felt a strong urge to "speak out" his response to what he saw. After some unsatisfying experiments with black and white, which he found cold and distant, he turned to color as a means of projecting warmth and providing viewers with a heightened sense of the physical presence of a scene.

Although he admires the work of Eliot Porter, Yuan Li's only teacher was the late Helen Manzer, whose classes he attended in New York City. "Mrs. Manzer made me aware of the need to give a photograph a well-defined and clearly stated theme," he says. His photographs have been published in *Arizona Highways* and *Camera 35*, among other magazines, and he has exhibited in New York, San Francisco, and Princeton. The photographs he took in 1980 on a visit to his native China created so much interest there that he was invited back as a guest of the Chinese Photographers Association.

Most of Li's landscapes were taken with a 35mm camera, usually with a zoom lens. He favors Kodachrome 64 for its warmth, and he does not use filters. He often uses a tripod to compose his pictures more carefully and ob-tain greater depth of field. He prefers late afternoon or early morning light because it provides better contrast and warmer tones, though on occasion an overcast sky or even a storm will help him create a dramatic image.

Although Yuan Li photographs other subjects, landscape provides him with the best opportunities to express the connection he feels between external nature and the inner spiritual world. And modern photography, "with its unique capability to reproduce what is in front of us in minute detail," is the ideal way to record "a fleeting moment that is captivating and inspiring."

In taking a picture he tries to steer a course midway between spontaneity and control. On the one hand, he says, a successful photograph must convey the impression that the photographer is in full control of what is in it. However, too much control can rob the picture of life. As he says, "Without emphasis or individual interpretation, landscape photography can be bland. In some way, this approach is influenced by my philosophy toward the land as an observer and interpreter, rather than a dictator and master."

Once he finds an area that appeals to him, he tries to let the landscape itself determine his approach to it. He often finds it necessary to go back frequently to a favored area because the first impression, though important, can be superficial. He compares this to a painter making several sketches before finding the right expression for a picture.

He often emphasizes the abstract element of landscape, for instance, by eliminating the horizon line and concentrating on the landscape below it. However, he does not insist that this approach is always the right one—even for himself. "Any creative process would cease to be creative if it became a routine repetition of fixed steps."

MOONRISE OVER MINGSHA DUNES, NEAR DUNHUANG, CHINA

Copyright 1983 by Yuan Li. Canon FT, Kodachrome 64, 80–200mm lens, 1/8 sec. at f/22
Poets have spoken of life as an oasis in the desert and as a brief day bounded by night. Both metaphors are given visual expression in this photograph of zigzagging sand dunes seen from a refreshing, green area. The pale moon hanging above the small peak of a dune indicates the coming of night.

DEL VAL HILLSIDE,
NEAR LIVERMORE, CALIFORNIA

Copyright 1977 by Yuan Li. Canon FT, Kodachrome 64, 200mm lens, 1/4 sec. at f/22
The gently rolling hill serves as a backdrop to the lone tree, and
its counterparts further downhill, creating a setting very much
reminiscent of a still life. Yuan Li's photography emphasizes his
interest in the abstract patterns of nature and the effects of light
and shadow on those shapes.

SPRUCE ON THE HILLSIDE,
NEAR MOSCOW, IDAHO

Copyright 1983 by Yuan Li. Canon FT, Kodachrome 64, 80–200mm lens, 1/8 sec. at f/22
The juxtaposition of near-horizontal and vertical lines in this
photograph reminds Yuan Li of a music score sheet. Movement—
or rhythm—is created by the judicious placement of trees amid
the enfolding hills. The trees—the notes—appear in rhythmic
patterns in a landscape that doesn't end.

FEEDING SHACK ON PASTURE,
NEAR LIVERMORE, CALIFORNIA

Copyright 1977 by Yuan Li. Canon FT, Kodachrome 64, 135mm lens, 1/8 sec. at f/22
The little shack as the subject of this photograph is irrelevant. It is
the lines of its roof and wood paneling, as well as the lines in the
surrounding landscape, that caught Yuan Li's interest. The various
textures, from very smooth to very coarse, heighten the impact
and visual interest of the photograph.

WINDMILL BY THE HILL,
NEAR LIVERMORE, CALIFORNIA

Copyright 1977 by Yuan Li. Canon FT, Kodachrome 64, 200mm lens, 1/4 sec. at f/22
The plowed hay field provided the background with an interesting
texture and the late afternoon sun defined its contours. A long
lens compressed the field, resulting in an abstract design. A
magenta filter adjusted the colors, and a very painterly
effect was created.

SPRING FIELD AFTER THE RAIN,
NEAR PETERS VALLEY, CALIFORNIA

Copyright 1982 by Yuan Li. Canon A-1, Kodachrome 64, 80–200mm lens, 1/30 sec. at f/22
The greatest influence on Yuan Li's work is probably his Chinese heritage. He approaches landscape photography as a subject for contemplation and a source of inspiration, as well as a means of expressing his own thoughts and feelings. Here, the delicate mood of this misty California landscape takes on a very Oriental feeling.

Opposite page

HIGHLINES ON THE HILL,
NEAR LIVERMORE, CALIFORNIA

Copyright 1980 by Yuan Li. Canon A-1, Kodachrome 64, 80–200mm lens, 1/15 sec. at f/22
Man's presence in this rolling landscape is intrusive, but by no means powerful enough to command. Many of Yuan Li's land-scapes convey a sense of mankind's smallness and insignificance in the face of nature. The pylon carrying power lines is dwarfed by its natural, and very lovely, surroundings.

WINTER CLOUDBURST,
NEAR NEWTON, NEW JERSEY

Copyright 1979 by Yuan Li. Canon FT, Kodachrome 64, 80–200mm lens, 1/125 sec. at f/16
Man imposes his fences on the land in order to divide it and to
discourage trespassing, but nothing can minimize the hearty and
glorious expanse of this landscape. The late afternoon sun
provides contrast and warm tones, but clouds above threaten
momentarily to eclipse the light.

Preceding page

YOSEMITE CLIFF IN WINTER, YOSEMITE
NATIONAL PARK, CALIFORNIA

Copyright 1979 by Yuan Li. Canon A-1, Kodachrome 64, 80–200mm lens, 1/15 sec. at f/22
The quality of the light can render the landscape warm or cold,
powerful or vague. In this scene, the sharp light of winter reveals
myriad cracks, crevices, and textures in this cliffside wall. Li sees
this image as a completely abstract representation of nature
in the form of three triangles.

MIST OVER TUSKEGEE LAKE, ALABAMA

Copyright 1976 by Yuan Li. Canon FT, Kodachrome 64, 19mm lens, 1/30 sec. at f/16
"When I see a landscape, I feel that there are so many poems in that landscape. So I write a poem about it, with my camera." Yuan Li was attracted at an early age to Chinese classical poetry, which often uses landscape to convey philosophical ideas. He uses photography in order to do the very same thing.

SMOG OVER SAN JOSE VALLEY,
FROM MT. HAMILTON, CALIFORNIA

Copyright 1979 by Yuan Li. Canon FT, Kodachrome 64, 80–200mm lens, 1/60 sec. at f/16
Fog and smog and all manner of mists have a tantalizing effect on
the landscape. Here, there's little to recognize but the black
mountain peaks, and, perhaps, a reference to Chinese classical
painting, a great influence on the style and philosophy of Yuan Li.

SONJA BULLATY

The varying effects of climate, weather, and season play a major part in establishing the mood of Sonja Bullaty's landscape photographs. In one, the blue mists of a northern forest soften the background against which lichen-covered tree trunks and tender spring greenery stand out. In another the crystal clear air of the American Southwest brings into sharpest focus every stain, crevice and color of a vertical canyon wall. In some, blazing autumn leaves or pastel-colored spring flowers dominate the scene. In others, winter snow whitens rocks, trees, and half-frozen waters, dramatizing while transforming their shapes.

In one striking shot, which was taken on the Scottish Isle of Skye, the weather itself is the principle subject of the picture. Over a hay field and a little white cottage, a rocky peak juts up against the sky. Behind the peak a huge bank of fog presses forward, already curling around the edges of the peak and threatening to engulf peak, house, and field in a pale purple mist. The horizontal lines of the fog bank and field echo one another, and the gloomy darkness of the land below the fog is full of foreboding.

Sonja Bullaty is best known as part of the team of Bullaty and Lomeo, and she and her husband, Angelo Lomeo, often work together out of their apartment overlooking Central Park in New York City or their country retreat in Vermont. But each came to photography by a different route. Bullaty was born in Prague, Czechoslovakia, where until age fourteen she lived the normal life of a well-to-do banker's daughter. Then, when the Nazis invaded, she was taken out of school because she was Jewish, and her father gave her a camera as a consolation.

She was the only member of her family to survive the war, and after the war she was taken on as an assistant by Joseph Sudek, Czechoslovakia's best known photographer, who taught her, she says, that "photography can be more than a profession, that it is a way of life." By the time she came to New York and met Lomeo, she was an experienced, though self-taught, photographer.

Together Bullaty and Lomeo have achieved great success. Their essays have appeared in most of the major photography magazines as well as in *Life*, *Horizon*, the *Audubon Tree Guide*, the *Time-Life Wilderness Series* and a book of their own, *Vermont in All Weathers*. Each photographer also works individually. Bullaty's work has been shown at the Metropolitan Museum of Art and the International Center of Photography, both in New York, and the Museum of Modern Art, São Paulo, Brazil.

Bullaty uses 35mm single-lens reflex cameras, usually (though not always) without a tripod, and she may use any lens from an extra wide angle to a zoom depending on the requirements of the picture. She works primarily in color, but she has worked extensively in black and white, and still does on occasion. She thinks of color and black and white as different but complementary means of expression, like orchestral and chamber music. Occasionally she uses a warming filter or an ultra violet or polarizing filter when working in the mountains, but she does not use filters to radically alter or distort nature's colors. "I prefer not to manipulate things," she says. "The world is exciting and to capture what is there is a tremendous challenge."

Although Bullaty photographs people and cities as well as landscape, landscape is for her "a very important way to express what I feel about the world. When you have seen the depths of horror, you are so much more responsive to enormous joy. I have often felt that the reason I celebrate life and beauty is precisely because I have seen so much pain and ugliness."

She enjoys photographing the landscape early in the morning and just before and after sunset. And while she prefers an overcast day for increased color saturation, she finds that there are landscapes that only come to life in the full sun. "It depends on what mood one is in or wants to express."

The seasons—"and there are many seasons," she says, "not just four"—are a subject of which she never tires. Summer is the most difficult season for her to photograph, while winter, when "everything is reduced to basics," is her favorite. She likes to come back, over and over again, to a familiar subject like the countryside of Vermont or New York City. But extensive travel has taught her to size up a new subject quickly, and to realize that a first impression can be as valid as one based on longer acquaintance. In any case she tries to approach each subject with an open mind. "Even if I go out there with a preconceived idea, what is out there in nature will determine the image."

ISLE OF SKYE, SCOTLAND

Copyright 1984 by Sonja Bullaty
In one brief moment, Bullaty has captured a powerful glimpse of forces of nature in relation to the land. The clouds parted briefly on a rain-swept day to allow this view of a fog-bound mountain, house, and field. The lines of the fog bank and mountain echo one another, while the land below is full of ominous foreboding.

SPRINGTIME IN THE SMOKIES

Copyright 1984 by Sonja Bullaty
Here, again, weather played a major role in establishing the mood
of this photograph of a mountain forest. The mist of an early
morning fog softened the background, against which lichen-
covered tree trunks and tender spring greenery stand out. An
overcast day can give way to very delicate results.

SPRING ON THE CHARLES RIVER, BOSTON, MASSACHUSETTS

Copyright 1984 by Sonja Bullaty
The importance of life is what Sonya Bullaty tries to impart in her photographs. Springtime, with its lovely pastels, is a time of awakening and renewal, a joyous season that beckons us to take time to enjoy the pleasures that life has to offer—and nature, of course, is foremost among those pleasures.

FRENCH FIELDS

This ribboned stretch of field, delicately colored by the spring, appears perhaps more exciting because of the inclusion of the small, crumbling shack, whose position in the photograph gives it prominence, indeed importance. Perfectly placed, the shack determined the image—and its impact and emotional expression.

HIGH SIERRA SUNRISE

Although Bullaty says that she finds summer the most difficult season to photograph, this field of flowers certainly captures the feeling of warmth and buoyancy so often present during this period of the year. Beauty and life are expressed eloquently in these blooming poppies feeding on the early morning light.

GRAND CANYON

"The decision to photograph a landscape is determined by the landscape itself—and decisions are subconscious responses to one's surroundings." It is no wonder that Bullaty chose to capture this majestic scene at a truly decisive moment—as the last bit of the day's light struck the canyon peaks.

Opposite page

CANYON WALL WITH TREE

"The crystal clean air of the American Southwest brings into sharpest focus every stain, crevice, and color of a vertical canyon wall." A detail can be just as powerful as a sweeping, all-encompassing landscape, and provides an opportunity to explore the make-up of a huge entity, here a canyon wall.

POND REFLECTIONS, VERMONT

Copyright 1984 by Sonja Bullaty

The great trees surrounding this pond are not photographed
directly, but their bushy shapes and blazing autumnal colors are
reflected strikingly in the water. The trees fill the upper portion of
the frame and provide a border—and a contrast to—the airy,
lower portion consisting of simple reeds.

AUTUMN IN THE MAINE WOODS

Copyright 1984 by Sonja Bullaty

All seasons have a personality and beauty all their own, but the fall, just before the deep sleep of winter, brings out an incredible display of maximum color. It was early in the morning when Sonja Bullaty set up her tripod and photographed this red sumac, simple in shape but exuberant in the midst of its quiet surroundings.

Overleaf

HIGH SIERRA POND

Copyright 1984 by Sonja Bullaty

Abstract patterns in nature enchant Bullaty, as do reflections in water and the further abstraction of those patterns. Here, the emphasis may be on the reflections and ice flow, but one's attention is equally divided between the canyon wall and the water.

ROCKS AND REDWOODS, HIGH SIERRA

Winter is the season most preferred for photographing by Sonja Bullaty, a season when "everything is reduced to basics." The structure of the land and the trees is revealed with a minimum of very important color, and winter snow, blanketing everything in sight, dramatizes while transforming nature's various shapes.

Opposite page

SPRING THAW, HIGH SIERRA

"The photographer," according to Bullaty, "should try to distill symbols so that the picture represents universality as much as possible." This photograph of deep winter snows giving way to spring is a fine illustration of Bullaty's words. Surely the idea of awakening could not be better expressed.

ANGELO LOMEO

There is often some sign of human occupance, some visible evidence that human beings live on the land and use it for their own purposes, in the landscape photographs of Angelo Lomeo. It may be a golden wheat field stretching across the high prairies of Montana where tall grasses once grew wild. It may be the low, crumbling walls of an old church sitting at the end of a sunflower field. It may be a sunny hillside dotted with stacks of new-mown hay and crowned with a low, rambling, tile-roofed house. Or it may be a road sign popping up unexpectedly in a landscape of primeval grandeur and desolation, a sign that seems busily self-important, almost absurd, compared to the rugged majesty of the landscape behind it.

On the whole Lomeo seems cheerful about man's presence in nature. Man often adds a new beauty to the landscape by planting fields of grain or flowers, and in Lomeo's photographs the roads are two-lane black tops that open up the countryside without destroying it. Even the road signs, with their bright primary colors and geometrical shapes, are subordinated to their natural surroundings. The yellow road sign at the bottom of the picture at right is small and inconspicuous. The picture is dominated by the snowy hillside and the thick forest of bare-branched trees. The sign is scarcely more than a humorous reminder that most people see this kind of landscape through the windows of a passing car.

Angelo Lomeo and his wife, Sonja Bullaty, travel and work together all over the world, and their photographs are usually presented with both their names on them. But each brings a distinct vision to the landscape. Lomeo, a second-generation American, grew up in an Italian-speaking household in New York City's Hell's Kitchen. He started photographing at the age of nine with a Kodak Brownie, and "from that moment on," he says, "it was magic."

Later he studied painting and design at New York's School of Industrial Art, but he was unwilling to spend the rest of his life in a design studio, and after military service in the Second World War he headed for the American West, lured by the legendary beauty of the landscape. While working as a lumberjack in Montana, he began taking photographs of the local scenery and selling them to tourists, and this success encouraged him to return to New York and pursue a professional career in photography.

As a team Bullaty and Lomeo have done everything from social documentary in the rural South to coverage of high life among the aristocrats of Britain. Although they dislike categories for their work, they are probably best known as travel and nature photographers, and their work has appeared in numerous magazines including *Life* and *Horizon* and leading photography magazines. They have done a book, *Vermont in All Weathers*, and have contributed extensively to the *Audubon Tree Guide* and the *Time-Life Wilderness Library*.

Lomeo works with a 35mm camera, usually hand held, and when on location he carries a wide assortment of lenses as well as a tripod for those occasions when he needs it. But he shoots sparingly. "I do not point the camera at a subject unless I feel strongly that there is something there that I must capture, not only for myself but for others to see. When you consider the actual number of rolls of film in a photographer's lifetime, you realize that the really successful images are comparatively few."

The greatest single influence on Lomeo's vision was the breadth and beauty of the western landscape as seen by a city boy used to cramped, narrow spaces, and he still likes to approach every landscape as simply and directly as possible. He uses filters only when necessary to counteract glare or cut through mists, and although he has worked extensively in black and white and learned a lot from it, he prefers color because, as he says, "the world is a colorful place."

Lomeo is a great admirer of the paintings of Edward Hopper, and claims Hopper's use of light as a strong influence. He still looks for the way light and shadows determine the outcome of the photograph. In fact, Lomeo sees the landscape as a great challenge to the photographer simply because of the constantly changing light. "To make a truly strong photograph of a landscape," he says, "I try to wait until all the conditions are right and can be distilled into the one moment."

ARROW IN WINTER, VERMONT

A colorful touch, courtesy of man, adds a highlight to this thick forest of bare-branched trees on a snowy hillside. The small yellow road sign, indicating a direction in opposition to the grand vertical landscape, typifies the wry humor and strong sense of design inherent in Angelo Lomeo's landscapes.

CURVED ROAD SIGN, BADLANDS,
SOUTH DAKOTA

A product of the city, Angelo Lomeo is quite taken by the breadth
and beauty of the western landscape. Once again, man's presence
in nature is marked, this time by a "curved road ahead" sign, a
warning that can serve also perhaps as an indicator of the jagged
shapes of the imposing landscape.

STOP SIGN, BADLANDS, SOUTH DAKOTA

Again, a sign pops up unexpectedly in a landscape of primeval grandeur—self-important and absurd compared to the rugged majesty of the landscape behind it. Why would a stop sign be required in this seemingly desolate area? Perhaps it should be interpreted as a demand to stop and admire the view.

AUTUMN ROAD, VERMONT

A two-lane road opens up the countryside without imposing on it.
The golden autumn vegetation bordering the road provides a tent-
like protective sheaf to the traveler's path on this evenly lit bright,
yet overcast day.

FRENCH ROAD

Neat rows of birch trees border and isolate a road in the rolling
French countryside, a road which leads, it seems, to an impending
rainstorm in the distance. Repeated vertical lines are a perennial
favorite of Lomeo's camera, not to mention conspicuous and not-
so-conspicuous road signs.

HOUSE ON HILL, TUSCANY

Copyright 1984 by Angelo Lomeo

In the lovely north of Italy, a hillside dotted with stacks of newly mown hay is crowned by a low, rambling, tile-roofed house. The knobby, gently rippling hillside adds a sense of atmosphere and beauty to the photograph, while the eerie, diffused light offered by the imminent storm adds great drama.

MONTANA WHEAT

Many of Angelo Lomeo's photographs are dominated by broad horizontal fields which constitute the greater portion of the picture frame. This golden wheat field, stretching across the high prairies of Montana, would be without end were it not for the thin, blue zigzags of mountains and sky.

Overleaf
SUNFLOWERS, FRANCE

Lomeo's landscape photographs often feature some visible evidence of human presence, whether it be of long ago or recent occupance. Here, an ancient, crumbling, abandoned church, seemingly protected by tall, ominous trees, is overpowered by the sprawling sunflower field bursting with life and color.

LAKE MacDONALD, MONTANA

Angelo Lomeo approaches every landscape as simply and as
directly as possible, and with a certain amount of reverence and
awe. Why manipulate the perfection that nature provides? Here, he
composes a striking image of patterns, a result of the early
morning light and the mountain reflections.

DEAD SEA, ISRAEL

The unusual salt formations in the waters of the Dead Sea attracted Angelo Lomeo's eye and camera. His image evokes an ancient time—appropriately, of course, for the Holy Land—but perhaps it also expresses a strange, other worldliness, an effect achieved in part by the harsh light of the blistering, mid-day sun.

BIRCH TREES, ACADIA, MAINE

The mighty white birch tree is the target of many of Lomeo's
photographs. His passion for trees began years before, when, as a
child, he discovered the charms of Central Park and, particularly,
of one old mulberry tree—his favorite haunt. Trees continue to
represent, for him, a sense of splendor and strength.

Opposite page

LARCHES, MONTANA

The strong, yet simple lines of the tree trunks in this photograph
express Lomeo's keen graphic and somewhat offbeat sense of
design, as well as his fondness for strictly vertical or horizontal
subjects. The misty morning sunlight imbued the proud, white
larches with a frail, skeletal quality.

FRANCO FONTANA

In Franco Fontana's landscapes, the infinite variety of the visible world is often reduced to a few bands of color harmoniously arranged within the picture space. In one view across a gently rolling field, a strip of gold divides two dark green areas from one another. The only other element in the picture is the pale blue, cloudless sky which fills the upper two thirds of the picture. In another, the photograph is divided almost in the middle, a golden field below, and above, a dark blue sky in which two white oval shapes, clouds, are stacked one above the other. In a third, a view across water, almost nothing is seen but a distant horizon line that divides two areas of opalescent blue.

These pictures, though minimal, are not abstract, for the photographer has captured the look and feel of the bit of nature that was in front of his camera when the exposure was made. And in some of his landscapes Fontana, without departing from the severe simplicity of his style, includes a little more of nature. In his first landscape, the picture is divided into three basic areas: sky blue, sand white, and earth brown. However, the brown of the earth is broken by furrows and patches of light, and in the right side of the picture a small tree, almost the color of earth, punctuates the otherwise empty field. In other pictures a row of trees, mirrored in water or dividing a green field from gold, marches across the picture as an element of the design.

Franco Fontana came to photography via the amateur camera club. A native of Modena in northern Italy, he was a successful dealer in high-style modern furniture when he took his first pictures. In the beginning he photographed sunsets and anything else in nature that he found beautiful in itself. Then he began to explore the textures of walls and windows of old buildings, things not necessarily beautiful in themselves but that could be made into beautiful pictures. Finally he came to see that anything could be the subject of a good photograph; what counted was what the photographer brought to it.

Fontana never studied art and he taught himself to be a photographer. However, he is now internationally known as an artistic photographer. He had his first one-man show in Modena in 1968, and has published several books of photographs, including a portrait of his city, *Modena una citta* (1971), and photographs of the Italian countryside *Terra de leggere* (1974). International recognition came when Fritz Gruber showed a group of Fontana's landscapes at the Photokina exhibition in Cologne, Germany. In 1976, Fontana gave up his business to devote himself to photography full time, and since then his photographs have been widely seen internationally in exhibitions and in publications including *Life* and Time-Life *Photography Year*.

He uses a 35mm single-lens-reflex camera and when photographing landscape he almost always uses a zoom lens. "This allows me to move easily, isolate the space according to my interpretation, and to give the landscape a two-dimensional impact, depriving it of all perspective." He always photographs in color because "when I open my eyes I see colors; for me it is natural to interpret reality as I see it." He does not use filters, but he does underexpose to improve color saturation. He photographs in all seasons, and likes the afternoon light on clear days for its warmth and for the contrasts between light and shadow which it creates.

The greatest influence on his work is, he says, "that great theater, the world. It provides an endless quantity of raw materials which I seek to interpret and give meaning to according to my view of reality." And when he has interpreted it, the world has an air of timeless universality. Even when cultivated fields are his subject, there are no tractors, paved roads, farm buildings or power lines to place them in the 20th century. They could be, he has said, from the world as it was 2,000 years ago, or they could be from the world of tomorrow.

He illustrates his approach to landscape by comparing the actual scene to be photographed to a sculptor's block of marble. "For a sculptor it is not the block of marble which determines his work. The marble is only the raw material, part of an insignificant reality. But by using the marble as a pretext, the sculptor brings the work into being, through style and creativity. This is my approach to landscape in general."

In addition to landscape he now photographs the human figure. "But my approach, that is, my personal style, doesn't change. No matter what the subject, I seek to delete everything that might render the picture too descriptive. A photograph is always an interpretation, not an illustration."

LUCANIA, (BASILICATA) REGION, SOUTHERN ITALY

Copyright 1978 by Franco Fontana. Canon A-1, Ektachrome 64, 85–300mm lens, 1/125 sec. at f/16
In this landscape, where the dominant color is the brown of the furrowed earth and the blue of the sky, one's eye is caught by the white dusty road that cuts through the ground like a wound, emphasizing and giving tension to the image.

BORGET LAKE, FRANCE

Copyright 1976 by Franco Fontana. Canon AE-1, Ektachrome 64, 100–200mm lens, 1/60 sec. at f/8
This perfect reflection provides a wonderful mirror-image composition.
To Fontana, this photograph recalls the archaic impressions of leaves,
in clear contrast to the descriptive reality of trees. It is a landscape
full of vitality and mystery.

Preceding page
SAN VALENTINO LAKE, EMILIA REGION, NORTHERN ITALY

Copyright 1978 by Franco Fontana. Canon A-1, Ektachrome 64, 20mm lens, 1/125 sec. at f/22
A very interesting ambiguity emerges from the contrast between
the form of the hill covered with snow and the blue of the sky.
The hill, mirrored in the reflection of the lake, is the determining
factor in the image's meaning. Fontana based his exposure on the
snow, consequently saturating the sky without the need of a filter.

LUCANIA (BASILICATA) REGION, SOUTHERN ITALY

Copyright 1978 by Franco Fontana. Canon A-1, Ektachrome 64, 85–300mm lens, 1/125 sec. at f/11
The varied areas of cultivation fit together in perfect harmony, conveying the dynamics of gentle movement, while the row of trees adds a sense of abstraction to the design. Fontana's images are often composed of such simple elements that they appear deceptively easy to realize. They are, of course, much more difficult to achieve.

LUCANIA (BASILICATA) REGION, SOUTHERN ITALY

Copyright 1975 by Franco Fontana. Canon F-1, Ektachrome 64, 100–200mm lens, 1/60 sec. at f/16

This photograph is another example of Fontana's rigorous, almost abstract composition. Notice the elegance of the lines, so prevalent in his landscapes. The calibrated intersection of the colorful rhombus of wild flowers work in harmony with the perfect lines of the hillside cultivation to soften the contrast.

LUCANIA (BASILICATA) REGION, SOUTHERN ITALY

Copyright 1978 by Franco Fontana. Canon A-1, Ektachrome 64, 85–300mm lens, 1/125 sec. at f/16
Beyond the immediate compositional value of the forms, Fontana
sensed the dimension of time. The emphatic contrast among the varied
tones of green and yellow gives a feeling of things continuously
changing, and the tree is like a fixed point, expressing a deep emotion
to be infinitely interpreted.

LUCANIA (BASILICATA) REGION, SOUTHERN ITALY

Copyright 1978 by Franco Fontana. Canon A-1, Ektachrome 64, 85–300mm lens, 1/125 sec. at f/16
Traces of life and signs of various forms of cultivation give form and substance to Fontana's way of interpreting the landscape. Like a magical presence, the red line of the poppies crosses the image at the center, as though they had come from far away to bear witness to their presence and being.

LUCANIA (BASILICATA) REGION,
SOUTHERN ITALY

Copyright 1975 by Franco Fontana. Canon F-1, Ektachrome 64, 100–200mm lens, 1/125 sec. at f/11
The yellow streaks across the field like a lash, as if to give life, meaning,
and force to the static meeting of the dark green and the blue sky. As
with so many of Fontana's photographs, it is a very concise image,
where less signifies more.

Overleaf

LUCANIA (BASILICATA) REGION,
SOUTHERN ITALY

Copyright 1978 by Franco Fontana. Canon AE-1, Ektachrome 64, 85–300mm lens, 1/125 sec. at f/22
A two-stop underexposure was used to make the sky seem more
looming over the black hill over the horizon, and above all to
emphasize the violence of the yellow as an emotional factor. The two
small clouds become barely perceptible, lending even greater ambiguity
to this extraordinarily natural scene.

WHITE SANDS, NEW MEXICO

Copyright 1982 by Franco Fontana. Canon F-1, Ektachrome 64, 24–35mm lens, 1/250 sec. at f/22
The strong, noon-day light creates the contrast in this image of an
enormous white sand dune reflected in a puddle of water from a recent
thunder storm. For Fontana, this is an image full of joy, where the
beauty of the "banal" is done justice.

Preceding page

ADRIATIC SEA, EMILIA-ROMAGNA REGION,
NORTHERN ITALY

Copyright 1975 by Franco Fontana. Canon F-1, Ektachrome 64, 20mm lens, 1/125 sec. at f/16
The apparent static design of this image becomes animated by the
sand, crisscrossed by footprints, and by the perpetual movement
of the waves. A sense of harmony is achieved by the contrast in
the dual elements of color and movement.

LAGOON AT COMACCHIO, EMILIA-ROMAGNA REGION, NORTHERN ITALY

Copyright 1976 by Franco Fontana. Canon AE-1, Ektachrome 64, 20mm lens, 1/125 sec. at f/22

Fontana finds this scene especially fascinating because, to him, it represents the dimension of time and infinity, where nothing can be taken away or added, where color exists without violence. For Fontana, this photograph represents the culmination of his investigations of synthesis and meaning in exterior form.

JOHN CHANG McCURDY

Photograph by Andreas Feininger

Ｗith a few well-chosen details and a minimum of color, John Chang McCurdy's landscapes suggest a mysterious world of peace and serenity. In one photograph in the following portfolio, a delicate tracery of brown, leafless stalks silhouetted against a background of white suggests the deep sleep of winter. In another, waves of white blossoms floating against a tangle of branches and tree trunks conveys the coming of spring. In a third, a symphony of buff and mauve, a few reeds trembling in the wind epitomize the quiet and beauty of the marshy areas where the land meets the sea.

In "Zen Pond," there is nothing shown but a faint reflection of a sunset sky in the pond's dark waters, as if sky and water had become one—that and a few reedy stalks in the foreground and a few lily pads higher up in the picture. The pond has no visible shore, the picture has no horizon line. The reeds and lily pads seem to float in an infinite space in the way that (we are told) all creation floats in eternity.

There is something oriental about the way these pictures suggest so much with such simple means, and indeed the photographer brings something of the orient to them. Though now an American citizen, John Chang McCurdy is Korean by birth and did not come to America until age thirteen, when he was adopted by an American family living in Berkeley, California. He was orphaned in the Korean War, which also nearly cost him his eyesight, and while still in Korea he bought his first camera at the age of eleven "to celebrate the gift of sight."

Once in the United States, he studied photography with Jack Welpott at California State University in San Francisco, then moved on to California State's extension at Uppsala University in Sweden, where he first studied and then taught. Recognition came at age twenty-five with an exhibition at the Museum of Modern Art, San Francisco, and after the publication in 1974 of his first book, *Of All Things Most Yielding* (McGraw-Hill), he became a freelance photographer for Time-Life Books. Since then he has published a book on Iceland in collaboration with Nobel laureate Haldor Laxness and exhibited widely in the United States and Scandinavia. He now lives in New York City where he does advertising and editorial photography. McCurdy feels that his work in advertising makes him more aware of details and nuances in nature that he had previously taken for granted.

In his commercial work McCurdy uses a wide range of cameras, lenses, filters and films according to the requirements of the job. But when photographing landscape, he prefers simple and light equipment, usually a 35mm single lens reflex or a 2¼-inch square Hasselblad. He often uses slow shutter speeds to achieve effects of movement—for example, the wind blowing through the reeds in "March Zephyr" and the overall agitation of "September Air." He prefers working in autumn for the color, and winter for the simplicity and likes to photograph early in the morning and late in the afternoon "when there are gentle colors and soft shadows. He does not use filters to change the colors of nature. "Most of the time I try to depict nature as it is," he says. In determining the qualities he likes to bring to the landscape, McCurdy says "Light and color must dance together."

McCurdy works in color rather than black and white because, as he says, "Color is for real, color is fun, color is life." Yet the range of colors he works in is often very narrow. Some of his pictures (for instance, "December" and "Dog Wood Forest") are almost monochromatic. Others, though more colorful, like "Vernal Slope" and "Autumn," have very little contrast between dark and light.

McCurdy also often finds a subject where others might see nothing but a confusion of shapes and colors. There is seldom a clearly defined center of interest, seldom a clearly articulated foreground, middle ground, and background. Instead, there is often an overall pattern in which many small shapes are repeated over and over again with tiny, barely perceptible variations.

These two characteristics of McCurdy's landscapes, their restricted color range and their overall pattern, work together to create an effect that verges on the mystical. Even in the most transient effects of nature—mists, reflections in water, the ripple of wind through grass—he seeks to show something that is universal and eternal. "For me a picture must have a spirit, a soul," he says. "The moment the spirit ceases to move it, it ceases to be a picture."

ZEN POND, SARANAC LAKES, NEW YORK

The deep purple hues of a sunset reflect in the still water, as a few reedy stalks and lily pads float in a seemingly endless space. With these few simple elements, McCurdy suggests a world of beauty in the landscape. It is his aim to imply the eternal element of the landscape in his work, as he does here with the minimal aspects of splendid design.

DECEMBER, BEAR MOUNTAIN, NEW YORK

Copyright 1979 by John Chang McCurdy. Hasselblad 2¼-inch SLR, Ektachrome Professional film

With this image, McCurdy shows the amount of design that can appear in an essentially monochromatic scene. The unusual composition includes a foreground that seems to exist on a single narrow plane, highlighted by the dramatic shape of the solitary black tree. Juxtaposed against the foreground is an unending distance of swirling snow drifts, adding, in its extreme contrast, an additional abstract element.

SNOW THISTLES,
BEAR MOUNTAIN, NEW YORK

In this view, a completely natural scene takes on the qualities of color and design that are more often associated with an abstract painting. In a snow-covered field, rows of bare branches stand in the background like matchsticks, while the foreground is splattered with the random arrangement of the thistles, adding an almost accidental touch of color to this winter landscape.

DOGWOOD FOREST, CONNECTICUT

Copyright 1979 by John Chang McCurdy. Hasselblad 2¼-inch SLR, 120 Ektachrome Professional film

It would seem almost impossible that the essence of the first blossoming of spring could be contained in this ivory landscape, yet the brilliant white flowers of the dogwoods seem to shimmer against the backdrop of a muted and misty forest. McCurdy often uses slow shutter speeds to show the natural movement of nature, and in this image he has captured the effect of gentle winds moving through the trees.

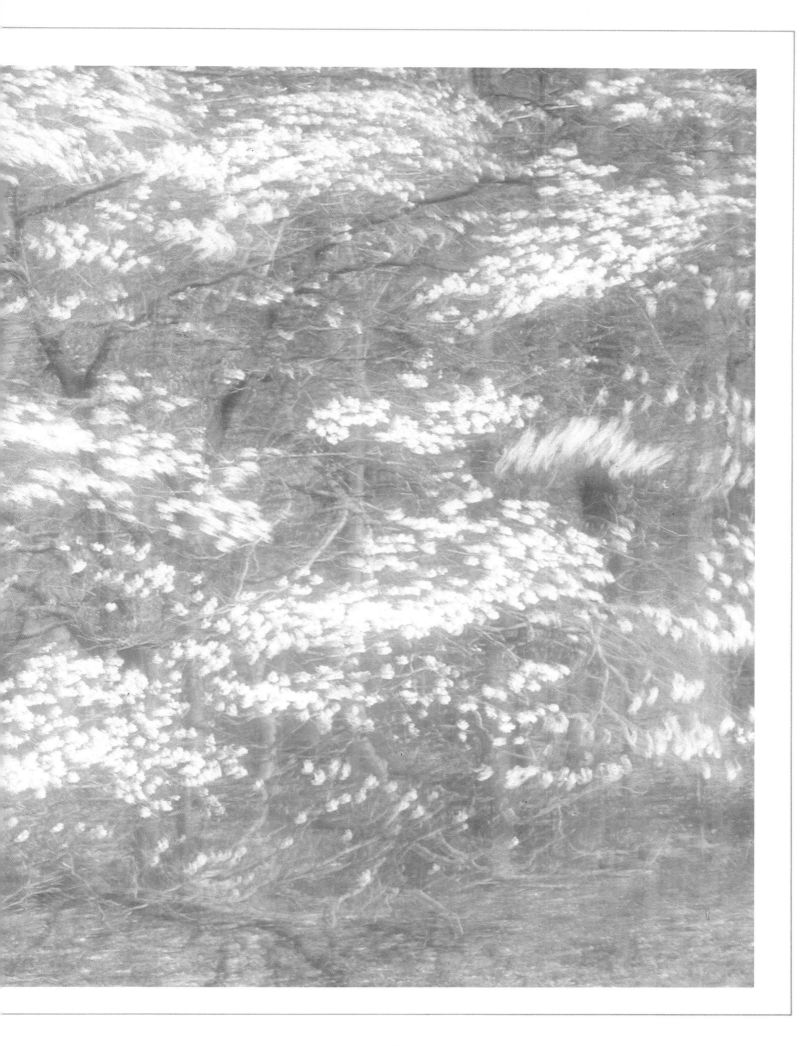

MARSH ZEPHYR, GILGO BEACH, LONG ISLAND, NEW YORK

Copyright 1979 by John Chang McCurdy. Hasselblad 2¼-inch SLR, 120 Ektachrome Professional film

Again, McCurdy uses a slow shutter to impart the natural movement of the tall grasses swaying in the ocean breeze. In addition, the slowed exposure gives a delicate, pastel shading to the muted colors of the seaside landscape. McCurdy creates a composition of patterns and contrasting shapes here, as the various bands of color in the background highlight the strict vertical repetition of the tall grass.

VERNAL SLOPE, SMOKY MOUNTAINS, SOUTHERN APPALACHIANS

Copyright 1979 by John Chang McCurdy. Hasselblad 2¼-inch SLR, 120 Ektachrome Professional film

The wonderful pastel shades of spring swirl together in this landscape, contrasted only by the singular lines of slim tree trunks and branches. As with so many of McCurdy's landscapes, there is no central subject to this image, no central point upon which one fixes the eye. Instead, the line of sight wanders over the image in a circular pattern, moving in rhythm with the patterns created by the colors.

MIST, SARANAC LAKES, NEW YORK

Copyright 1979 by John Chang McCurdy. Hasselblad 2¼-inch SLR, 120 Ektachrome
Professional film

McCurdy normally takes a comparatively close-up view of the
landscape, but here we have the definite impression of a broad
expanse of lake and shore hovering beyond the brilliantly colored
mist. A subtle sense of graphic design is also present, as band after
band of color stacks horizontally one on top of another.

SEPTEMBER AIR, ICELAND

Copyright 1979 by John Chang McCurdy. Hasselblad 2¼-inch SLR, 120 Ektachrome Professional film

This delicate view brings forth a landscape reminiscent of an Impressionist painting, or the early photographic landscapes of Edward Steichen. Again using a slow shutter speed, McCurdy creates an eerie atmosphere that simultaneously bursts forth with color. As splashes of multicolored flowers hold the foreground, a clearing gives way to straight rows of ominously dark trees.

AUTUMN, ADIRONDACK REGION, NEW YORK

Copyright 1979 by John Chang McCurdy. Hasselblad 2¼-inch SLR, 120 Ektachrome Professional film

In this image the brilliant colors of these two resplendent trees merge across an open space, and the very air seems to crackle with the crisp light of the fall season. Again, there is no central subject, no foreground or background plane to catch the viewer's eye, only the colors and forms of the landscape in natural motion.

STEVEN C. WILSON

The way animals, plants, and people live in a wilderness environment is the subject of the following photographs by Steven C. Wilson, most of which were taken in the desolate grandeur of Alaska's remote but beautiful Aleutian Islands chain. In one, sunlight breaks through gathering storm clouds and touches the rocky peak where sea gulls stand guard over their nests and eggs. In another, a northern sea crashes against jagged rocks under clouds that hide snow-covered mountain tops.

In the opening photograph, sea lions bask in the sunlight on the black sands at the base of a rocky cliff. The cliff rises up from cold, black waters on the surface of which ice is floating, and every ledge and crevice is green with low-growing mosses.

The sea and its creatures have enthralled Steven Wilson ever since he was young, and after two years as a student at the Los Angeles Art Center he majored in marine biology at the University of Washington School of Fisheries. "I figured it was important to know something about the insides of what I planned to photograph the outsides of," he says. At the beginning of his professional career he did some industrial photography and a number of annual reports, but success has enabled him to pick and choose his assignments. He now works mainly for organizations such as the National Geographic Society.

Wilson often spends long periods in the field, and his equipment reflects this fact. "I have three backpacks of gear, one that is waterproof and floats, one that is dust- and snow-proof and is insulated against heat and cold, and one that is elegant enough to carry into a CEO's inner sanctum." He uses 35mm cameras with a wide range of lenses and a tripod is always attached to the camera, even if its feet don't touch the ground—"just for extra weight to dampen the mirror slap." Other equipment includes A-2 filters on every lens except his 15mm, 2 × 2 gels (used on occasion for balancing light), and a Pentax Spotmeter for checking contrasts. He uses mirrors, both flat and concave, to supplement direct sunlight, since batteries may go bad after a long time in the field, and is prepared if need be to trigger his cameras by remote control with an infra-red beam or sound tripper, meanwhile watching both his cameras and his subject with shielded binoculars.

Steve Wilson is as much a scientist as he is a photographer, and his primary aim as a scientist is to capture on film information about the relationships between living creatures and their environments. He calls himself a "habitat photographer" rather than a landscape photographer, but he often has to back away from his subjects to show them and their environment in a true relationship.

Wilson photographs in all seasons and at whatever time of day "the normal inhabitants of the landscape are up and about." Here he is speaking as a scientist, but as a photographer, he says, it is not the subject he has to capture on film, but the light reflected from the subject. "I try to cooperate with the quality of light so it simplifies the *visual* relationship yet reinforces the basic insight of the photograph." Like other scientists before him, he is more interested in getting his story told than in maintaining photographic purity. Thus he is perfectly willing to combine two slides—for example, a slide of the environment "at its most transparent" with a slide of the animal "when most gainfully employed"—when he cannot get the whole story of the animal in its environment in a single exposure. Similarly, he uses color film rather than black and white because, for one thing, professional color processors save him the time and trouble of darkroom work. "Sure I could get a bit more 'Wilson-in-the-photograph' by doing it myself, but I invest that time in more 'before-the-shutter-is-punched' research."

At the heart of Wilson's achievement is his love of his subject matter. "For Steve a subject is not a subject, it's a religion," one of his picture editors has said. To him, the landscape is a constantly changing, living environment—but because these changes occur so slowly, we, as observers, don't always take notice. The purposeful frame of Wilson's photographs—intimate detail in the foreground coupled with an expansive background—is intentionally designed to make the viewer aware of the landscape as a habitat, a place where living creatures coexist with their surroundings.

SEA LION ROOKERY, CAPE MORGAN, AKUTAN ISLAND, ALEUTIAN ISLANDS

Copyright 1983 by Steven C. Wilson/ENTHEOS. Nikon F, Kodachrome 64, 105mm lens, 1/60 sec. at f/11
With an appropriately timeless view, Wilson depicts the habitat of the Aleutian island chain. In this early morning scene, the water meets almost directly with the jutting cliffs, showing the elements that have fostered an abundant population of marine wildlife.

CORMORANT-SEA GULL ROOKERY, NEAR UNGA ISLAND, ALEUTIAN ISLANDS

Copyright 1983 by Steven C. Wilson/ENTHEOS. Nikon F, Kodachrome 64, 15mm lens, 1/250 sec. at f/22

The dramatic lighting of an oncoming storm heightens the impact of this spectacular photogrpah. Wilson stalked this rookery for five days, watching the scene with binoculars from a boat, while three cameras with infra-red remote trippers stood waiting at the site. The deliberate emphasis in the foreground, coupled with the broad, sweeping background view give clarity to Wilson's idea of the landscape as a total environment.

WILLOW TREES, AKUN ISLAND,
ALEUTIAN ISLANDS

Copyright 1983 by Steven C. Wilson/ENTHEOS. Nikon F, Kodachrome 64, 15mm lens, 1/60 sec. at f/22

The element of survival, so prevalent in an area such as the Aleutians, is aptly depicted in this seemingly barren landscape. It is often said that there are no trees in the Aleutians, yet these gnarled willows prove otherwise. By clinging low to the ground, they protect themselves from the fierce, constant winds, which would otherwise strip them of their bark.

SEA LIONS, BISHOP POINT, UNALASKA ISLAND, ALEUTIAN ISLANDS

Copyright 1983 by Steven C. Wilson/ENTHEOS. Nikon F, Kodachrome 64, 55mm micro lens, 1/125 sec. at f/16

A playful juxtaposition of shapes highlights the wildlife of the Aleutian Islands against the forbidding landscape. Wilson took this photograph from a small boat off shore, coming in low enough to enable him to silhouette the group of sea lions against the snow-covered backdrop of mountains.

Preceding page

OLYMPIC NATIONAL FOREST, WASHINGTON

Copyright 1984 by Steven C. Wilson/ENTHEOS. Nikon F, Kodachrome 64, 15mm lens, 1 sec. at f/22

This ravaged landscape stands as dramatic evidence of man's destructive influence on his environment. This scene would at first appear to be the site of some natural devastation, when in actuality, a once majestic forest has been felled for lumber export. Once again, Wilson's purposeful use of the foreground heightens the impression of the broad expanse of what once existed.

OKMOK CRATER, UMNAK ISLAND, ALEUTIAN ISLANDS

In striking contrast to Wilson's usual view of the landscape full of life, this vast, unvegetated caldera provides an image that is alive with shapes and textures of a truly natural environment. This monochromatic scene takes on a strong graphic element as the design of the snow and ice against the black earth continues into a distance that seems without end.

MOUNT VSEVIDOF, UMNAK ISLAND, ALEUTIAN ISLANDS

Copyright 1983 by Steven C. Wilson/ENTHEOS. Nikon F, Kodachrome 64, 55mm micro lens, 1/250 at f/32

Brilliant sunlight highlights the textures of the snow, giving further emphasis to this isolated peak. Frozen and foreboding, it looms large against the misty blue backdrop of the sky, giving true definition to the word "pinnacle."

ENTERING CHERNOFSKI HARBOR, UNALASKA ISLAND, ALEUTIAN ISLANDS

Copyright 1983 by Steven C. Wilson/ENTHEOS. Nikonos camera, Ektachrome 200, 28mm lens, 1/500 sec. at f/16

One of the most impressive things about the Aleutian Islands, according to Wilson, is that there is frequently no shoreline—just sea, snow, and mountains. Here he shows the marriage of these elements, where mountains of water meet mountains of rock, in an eloquent pictorial design.

Overleaf

SANDY BEACH CAMP, ALEUTIAN ISLANDS

Copyright 1983 by Steven C. Wilson/ENTHEOS. Nikon F, Kodachrome 64, 15mm, 1/15 sec. at f/22

A strong sense of visual design is always in evidence in Wilson's photographs. Here, the lovely reflection of a summer hunting camp at twilight forms a strong graphic image. The sharp yet subtle lighting creates a combination of dark, mysterious shapes and soft highlights, giving extra dimension to a quiet landscape.

CHILD'S GRAVE, ABANDONED VILLAGE OF KASHEGA, ALEUTIAN ISLANDS

Copyright 1983 by Steven C. Wilson/ENTHEOS. Nikon F, Kodachrome 64, 15mm lens, 1/30 sec. at f/22

This pastoral scene, almost painterly in its use of light and symbolism, reflects the passing of the Russian culture in the Aleutians. The stillness of the early morning light highlights the central foreground elements and combines with the vast background landscape to form an image filled with quiet emotion.

RED WING BLACKBIRD, THEODORE ROOSEVELT NATIONAL MONUMENT, NORTH DAKOTA

It is Wilson's intent to make the landscape come alive in his photographs. And even when that landscape is the northwestern Badlands, he gives us a vibrant image, filled with living and interacting creatures. Wilson designs his photographs around these ideas, and his love for the environment becomes an integral element in every frame he takes.

SHINZO MAEDA

In Shinzo Maeda's lyrical landscapes, the natural beauty of the Japanese countryside as it changes from season to season is shown in pictures of poetic delicacy. From the pale pink sprays of cherry blossoms, contrasted with plume-like fronds of bamboo bowed down by spring rains to an alpine torrent fed by the melting snows of June plunging downward through glistening rocks and towering evergreens; through a temple garden, where red and gold autumn leaves carpet the ground surrounding lichen-covered tree trunk to a forest where ice covers the bare branches of trees, shining in the sunlight against a dark sky—Maeda expresses the passage of time across the land with serene eloquence.

The quiet beauty of these photographs is typified by the opening photograph, which shows flowering fruit trees hanging like cobwebs between tall, sturdy evergreens. Backlighting heightens the contrast between the delicate pinks and yellows of the fruit trees and the dark greens of the conifers, while the lack of any definite center of interest—a frequent characteristic of

Maeda's pictures—directs the viewer's attention to the more abstract elements of color, texture, and pattern.

Shinzo Maeda was a lover of nature before he was a photographer, and it was a hiking trip through the mountains of his native Japan taken when he was 33 years old that led him to make his first attempts to express nature's beauties photographically. Another twelve years passed before he founded a photo agency and became a full-time professional, but since then he has become well-known in Japan and other countries. He has published eight books of his photographs, the most recent of which, *A Tree, A Blade of Grass* was published in Japanese and English in 1983. He has had many exhibitions of his work in Japan and has also exhibited at the Photokina in Cologne, Germany in 1978 and in Europhoto in Majorca, Spain in 1980.

Most of Maeda's landscape photographs, including all that are shown in the following portfolio, were taken with large-format view cameras rather than a 35mm single-lens reflex. He seldom uses filters, preferring to work with nature's own colors. Though he photographs in all seasons and all lights, he favors the warm light of morning and evening and the soft light of cloudy or rainy days. His favorite season is autumn for its melancholy atmosphere; after that, spring for its flowers and fresh green trees.

Maeda has never had any formal training in photography. "The camera will do the work by itself," he says, "so I don't have to be taught by others or study photography from a book." He does not think formal training is necessary for landscape photography "if you admire nature and have talent." Neither does he look to other photographers or painters as models, though some of his photographs are reminiscent of paintings. He himself has described his photograph of an ice-covered lake (page 141) as reminiscent of Japanese paint-

ing, and some of his other photographs, with their all-over patterns of color and shapes, recall the abstract paintings of Europe and America as well as Japan.

To Maeda, nature is teacher and model enough. And though he concentrates on the landscape of his native Japan, the geographical diversity of this island country gives him a wide range of natural features and climates to select from. Many of his pictures are taken in the Tokyo suburb of Hachiōgi, which he calls his home town. But others are taken as far away from home as Hokkaido.

Wherever he goes, Maeda tries to approach the landscape with an open mind. What he wants to convey to the viewer is "the marvelous moment when I encounter nature without any fixed idea or preconception." At the same time, however, he feels that a photographer has to have a philosophical view of life that is reflected in his work. Without this, his photographs will lack distinction.

Maeda's photographs have been compared to the traditional kind of Japanese poem called the *haiku*, usually a brief description of nature in which "a moment is grasped, a flash of something larger, something deeper." And there is certainly something about his photographs that suggests this form of poetry. By and large he avoids long views of famous beauty spots or spectacular scenes in favor of medium-range or close-up views of smaller segments of nature. Only one photograph in the following portfolio shows many miles of countryside. Most of the others have subjects that are at most a few hundred yards from the cameras. There is also never any sign of human habitation or occupation, even when the pictures are taken in suburban areas of (as in one photograph in the following collection) in the courtyard of a temple. Nature is left to speak as if mankind did not exist, and she speaks in the short but suggestive lines of the *haiku*.

FRUITFULNESS BETWEEN TREES, SUZUKO TŌGE, SHIGA

Copyright 1981 by Shinzo Maeda. Toyo Field 8×10 camera, Ektachrome E6, 600mm lens, ½ sec. at f/45

The scenery of Japan can appear comparatively quiet, but at certain times of the year, the land abounds with subtle colors in a variety of hues. This mountain's trees are not yet fully green, but the delicate pastel flowers indicate that winter is over, and spring has arrived. With Maeda's straightforward view, the eye is not directed to one particular area of the scene, but allowed to wander over the variety of textures and shapes.

CHERRY BLOSSOMS AND BAMBOO TREES, KAMIONKATA AT HACHIOGI-SHI, TOKYO

Copyright 1983 by Shinzo Maeda. Linhof Super Technika V 4×5 camera, Ektachrome E6, 400mm lens, 1 sec. at f/22

The misty atmosphere of a rainy day emphasizes the lushness of a bamboo forest. The lovely pink splash of cherry blossoms heightens the feeling of spring and adds to the graceful, natural design of the Japanese landscape that Maeda finds particularly appealing. He often photographs on rainy or overcast days, as the soft, even lighting gives a special quality to the colors and mood.

WET GRASSLAND, SHUNKUNITAI, HOKKAIDO

Copyright 1981 by Shinzo Maeda. Toyo Field 8×10 camera, Ektachrome E6, 300mm lens, ½ sec. at f/45

The vitality and natural, fluid movement of the landscape is aptly shown in this image of a northern Japanese grassland. In this treasured sanctuary for plants and wildlife, the summer sunlight brings out the textures of the grasses, emphasizing the wonderful variety of shapes and color gradations present in just a small portion of the landscape.

AWESOME STREAM, SUGOROKUDANI

Copyright 1982 by Shinzo Maeda. Linhof Super Technika V 4×5 camera, Ektachrome E6, 400mm lens, 1 sec. at f/32

In this powerful image of a landscape filled with the motion of rushing water, rocks and trees remain steadfast against the torrents. Maeda took this photograph in the rain to add further emphasis to the drenched rocks.

Opposite page

WATERFALL, KIJIMA-MURA, NAGANO

Copyright 1980 by Shinzo Maeda. Toyo Field 8×10 camera, Ektachrome E6, 300mm lens, 1 sec. at f/32

Streams and waterfalls are among Maeda's favorite photographic subjects. He likes to bring a gentle feeling to these naturally spectacular scenes, and often chooses to photograph on a cloudy day rather than a bright one.

FLOWING LEAVES, KAMIKOCHI, NAGANO

Copyright 1982 by Shinzo Maeda. Linhof Super Technika V 4×5 camera, Ektachrome E6, 150mm lens, 1 sec. at f/22

Winter comes early to the mountains of Japan and here Maeda captures the last brilliant glow of autumn color. As the larch leaves flow gently down the current of a small stream, their movement creates a sweeping vision. Like so many of Maeda's gentle landscapes, it is a simple scene that implies a much greater spirit.

FULL-COLORED AUTUMN, SHIRAITONO-TAKI, URABANDAI, FUKUSHIMA

Copyright 1983 by Shinzo Maeda. Linhof Super Technika V 4×5 camera, Ektachrome E6, 400mm lens, 1 sec. at f/32

This area of Japan is well known for its opulent autumn foliage and Maeda photographs there often. As with waterfalls, he feels that red leaves are best photographed on cloudy days to obtain the most accurate color rendition. Once again, the entire view becomes the subject of our vision, as the spectacular collection of shapes and textures play against one another.

FALLEN MAPLE LEAVES, TAKAYAMA-SHI, GIFU

Copyright 1981 by Shinzo Maeda. Linhof Super Technika V 4×5 camera, Ektachrome E6, 90mm lens, 1 sec at f/22

Maeda feels that the Japanese landscape is at its most beautiful in autumn, and the subject of the fallen leaves is often celebrated in native poem and song. Wanting to imply the depth of the scenery in a temple garden, he photographed from a low angle, showing the viewer a gold and red carpet that trails far off into the distance.

CORAL PLANTS, NOTORO-KO, ABASHIRI-SHI, HOKKAIDO

Copyright 1980 by Shinzo Maeda. Linhof Super Technika V 4×5 camera, Ektachrome E6, 150mm lens, ¼ sec. at f/32

In September, the coral plants in the Notoro lake turn bright red, making the water appear as if it were covered by a crimson blanket. Using diagonal lighting, Maeda was able to emphasize the detail of the plants, while creating the unusual mixture of textures and highlights on the water's surface.

THIN ICED FOREST, KAMIKOCHI, NAGANO

Copyright 1982 by Shinzo Maeda. Linhof Super Tecknika V 4×5 camera, Ektachrome E6, 250mm lens, ½ sec. at f/22

Maeda feels that the scenery can appear lonesome as autumn turns to winter and the trees lose their leaves. But then, a world of fantasy takes over as the thin ice decorates the barren branches like so many tiny flowers. In an image that is essentially monochromatic, Maeda captures the cool quality of the light in winter as it radiates from the crystallized forest.

ICED LAKE, MATSUMOTO, NAGANO

Copyright 1980 by Shinzo Maeda. Linhof Super Technika V, 4×5 camera, Ektachrome E6, 400mm lens, 1/8 sec. at f/32

For Maeda, the snow and ice of winter can change a scene dramatically, and he often finds that an otherwise ordinary view takes on new interest at this time of year. This striking image of a snow-covered lake is unusual and abstract in its composition, but to Maeda, it is reminiscent of Japanese paintings.

LAKE TAISHO AND HODAKA
MOUNTAINS, KAMIKŌCHI, NAGANO

Copyright 1982 by Shinzo Maeda. Linhof Super Technika V 4×5 camera, Ektachrome E6, 125mm lens, 1/8 sec. at f/22

When Maeda came upon the lake partially covered with snow, he knew that he wanted to photograph it as a scene emblematic of the northern Japanese landscape. But he waited for the perfect moment, when the sun dipped down below the western mountains and turned the water's surface silver, to emphasize the solemn atmosphere of the scene.